The Love Cycle

Destiny Wertz

BookLeaf Publishing

India | USA | UK

Presentation by *BookLeaf Publishing*

Web: www.bookleafpub.com

E-mail: info@bookleafpub.com

ISBN: 9789358312256

First edition 2023

*To my Mimi-- whose love is gone but not
forgotten*

ACKNOWLEDGEMENT

Thank you so much to my family, friends, my partner, and all my mentors who have helped to guide me and make this publication possible. I hope I've made you proud.

Seedling

A seed in shade will never bloom,
silent soil entrapping eager sprout.
I want us to be a flower,
but she will not give me sun.

I am drowning in over waters,
engulfed in yearning to break the surface.
Without light, I will soon die,
and with me, a part of my soul.

The earth will not sustain me much longer,
and some days, trying feels much harder than
perish
Heavenly glow will never glisten upon my
shrouded infant leaves from here
I am immovable.
I wanted only for us to be a flower, but some
dreams are made to die.

Drought

She is rain, and I like that.
After a most trying drought of a day, she is most
welcome.
Her loving showers cultivate sproutlings
awaiting bloom
She nourishes the earth with her embrace
Though the best part is at the end,
when her rain brings the brightest arch of color
and I, the flower, am reunited with my
on-again-off-again, the Sun
For awhile, the world seems better
She is rain, and I love that

Contemplation

I had not known forbidden fruit until I met you.
Your round figure hangs low on a delicate
branch,
poised mere inches from my nose, and I am
tempted.

My stomach grumbles, as I am famished.
Have been for a long time.
Maybe just a light snack.

Every time I lay my eyes upon your beauty,
I must stop myself from touching you,
holding you, loving you the way I desire to.

I want to run my fingers across your smooth
flesh,
kiss you goodnight every time we part, but more
than anything,
I want to show you real love, like some modern
Disney Princess shit.

I find myself quietly admiring how your skin
glows in the sun
how your caring touch, in my hands, along my
cheekbones,

makes my heart feel both like a sinking rock and
floating driftwood.

Any other apple, I would not hesitate for,
but this one, you, could be the last fruit I eat.
You will either be my delight, or my demise.

And I'm not sure I'm ready to risk the bite,
not yet.

She will never love me (and so...)

On sunny days, when golden rays illuminate her
sugar cookie sweet locks,
I desire nothing more than to weave my fingers
in, tickle the back of her neck with my pinkies,
and pull her close, feeling the pulsing, intimate,
electromagnetism between us as our lips meet
and perform Muzetta's Waltz until our lungs can
no longer hold breath.

At night, I imagine her soft form next to me,
perfectly perched on her side, awaiting my
delicate touch as my hand falls to rest in a sweet
spot just below her breast, where my thumb will
subconsciously sweep to and fro just above her
sensitive stomach until I drift off to sleep with
my nose nuzzled in the crook of her neck,
nostrils filled with the sugary scent of
wildflowers, feeling more at home holding her
than I have in all my life.

In the moments before I wake, my synapses fire
and flutter with thoughts of showing every inch
of her velvet skin my devotion with sprinkles of
kisses up and down each crevice of her sculpted

body until I find her center and can overwhelm her system with the same endorphins and affection that mine has for her, allow her to feel every sensation of my love on each individual nerve she possesses, to make my passion tangible.

During brief moments of the day, her being enters my conscience like a freight train, flashes of her smile and our former fleeting touches jumpstart my heart, urging it to break through my chest cavity and palpitate in her hand to the beat of her favorite songs, her warmth and glow radiating across the distance between us to meet my soul in its tepid, stagnancy and re-invigorate it with jazzy effervescence, further confirming to me that now that I've leapt from love's fateful edge, I don't know how I could ever stop falling.

The Ocean

I am drowning.

I am drowning in your ocean
Of anxiety,
Worry,
Selfishness,
And doubts

I am 7 feet under,
The water pressure increasing,
Pushing me further from the surface.

I can see the sun,
The sky,
Above me.

I fight for air,
Only managing small inhalations
At a time.
Each breath becomes
Less and less fulfilling,
As I've been underwater
For far too long.

I can hear those who care,

Shouting at me from the shore.
They tell me to get out of the sea,
To come to land.

In the ocean,
I have you.
I have both the fresh air of the surface,
And the heart-shattering panic
Of your water filling up my lungs.

Upon the shore,
I am dry.
I am safe.
I can breathe with ease.
I am alone.

You are so far away.
And I know what happens
If I were to go back.
The ocean would unleash
Its wrath,

And I would never survive.

And so I stay in the ocean,
Where each breath
Is an exhausting battle.

I suppose I'd rather drown,
Than to risk the pain
Of swimming away.

Because as you know,
Once you fall in love with the ocean,
It will always call to you

Thunder

With the day having come and gone, I am
regretful.
I wish that I could take it all back, take that night
back.
Those three words should have never left my
lips. To see the flash of panic in your eyes,
I knew I'd made a mistake, tarnished a cloth,
said something I couldn't un-say.
I keep wanting things to go back to normal,
whatever that is.
But what even was normal for us?

When we met, I knew you would be special,
I knew I would fall for you before I even really
knew you
and then you laid your head on my chest, placed
your hand in mine,
I hoped you couldn't hear my increased heart
rate or my internal shrieks
I was in the eye of the storm that had been on
the horizon for quite awhile.

Now, I find myself biting my tongue, avoiding
your eyes,

clutching my pinky fingers into my hand until
they turn purple.
I feel foolish for having hope, for having
feelings at all.
Sometimes I think things would be better if I
blew away with the wind.

All I do now is lay in my bed, replaying my
every error in my mind.
I pray this ache in my chest is just a bruise, and
not a break,
for I cannot afford to fix my broken self again.

Price Tag

Somedays, it feels like I am only worth whatever
my organs would sell for on the black market
Like there is no value to my mind, spirit, or soul
No, all of that comes included in the $150 cost
of my brain
And that's tax-free

On the days when I feel ugly, I wonder if
someone else would be more beautiful in my
skin,
If they'd be getting the bang for their buck at
$10 per square inch,
If I sold my corneas for $15,000 a pop,
Would they see the same demons I do everytime
I close my eyes?

I was gifted this body by the miracle of birth,
But all I do is waste time, waste space, waste a
$157,000 liver I hardly even use
Because despite how fucked up I am,
I don't even drink

No, instead I live with a pain no can even
describe

My feet are heavy and swollen with the labors of
my mind,
is there something wrong with my kidneys,
God I hope not, they're $200,000 each
They're practically all I'm good for

The human body is worth $525,224 when
broken down and sold for its parts
Today, I feel I am only worth that much
Today, I hope my heart has a good selling price
Because it cost me everything

Taste of You

When I come home each day, my favorite thing
is you
For hours, I sit at my desk, longing for when
we'll meet again
My core aches when we're apart, like you're a
drug, and I'm in withdrawal

The second I step through the door, I need a hit
I crash onto your lips, don't even register the
thud of your spine against the wall
Too consumed in your taste, in the softness of
your flesh,
in the fresh scent of morning glories radiating
from your hair
You drive me wild, baby.

My hands find your hips, the hem of your shirt,
break the kiss just long enough to free you of it
Hooking thumbs under waistbands, I dispose of
your cloth cage
Relishing in your plush skin under my fingertips

Feels too good, can't process it
Lay you down, peel you open,
consume you in a way only I can

your symphony of ecstasy echoes through the
room,
I'm high

Love

Quick to jump in, but fast to deny,
breathing while burning would carry a kinder
vex.
Seconds become agonizing,
minutes are torturous.

Kisses and quiet whispers are the heartbeat,
giving life, pulling weight, clutching at finite
strings,
brazen sentiments fueling desire
but beware a wicked jynx

A double-edged sword almighty ablaze,
capable of melancholy and of climax
For kings and queens alike it is,
though it may be quite the journey

Inspiration of joy and transmission of sorrow,
your quaint world is a canvas for it,
juggling saturations from bright Xanthic to
kitschy Zunisha,
paint your cosmos in color, don't mind any
chaos

Exhale

Her smile feels like cool shower after a hot day
Her laugh a symphony for one
Her touch an exhale after years of holding my
breath

With her, I am a sailboat,
floating on the sea's gentle waves
She is my wind,
keeping me moving and alive

In her arms, I have never felt more free
and I have never breathed so easy

Fear

The light grows closer,
The shadow fades.
My shelter weakens,
My time grows short.
Extension of timid paw,
Seering, seething, burning fur.
The sun is too bright, too hot,
I am cornered by the rays.
Soon, I will run out of darkness,
And the blaze will eat me alive.

Insecurity

19

Am I good enough?
If not, will I ever be?
What if I don't care?

Blossom

She rescued me from the flowerbed,
potted me tight and took me home.
She plucked my wilting petals
and nurtured damaged roots

She put me in the perfect place,
a bay window where the sun always hit just
right,
She never forgets about me,
even when she is away.

She saved my life,
she made me better,
she has been nothing but patient and kind

I repay her in the only way I know how,
with fresh air, new life,
and hope

Sunflower

We are young sunflowers in the wind,
petals catching the summer breeze
causing our stems to shake

We've endured the brutal season side by side,
through whipping gales and heaving downpours
Yet together, we still stand

Even when a neighbor tree stood so tall
that it shaded all our sun,
we turned to one another

We have found solace in centers,
sharing energy for survival,
flourishing in synchronicity

Compliments

When I am with you, I feel beautiful
For others, that may not mean much, but to me,
it is the world

When I tell you that you're pretty, your response
is always the same:
A dismissive chuckle and "I'm just me."

But you are extraordinary, my love
You give me courage in ways I couldn't even
imagine

When I am with you, I'm no longer the big girl
The pounds of weight and shame shed
themselves from my mind,

I can hold your hand in public, lay sprawled
across your chest
Feel sexy in both lingerie and in the baggiest
clothes I own

And I am "just me," momentarily the center of
your world.
Then your hand clenches mine, squeezes three
times

And we kiss.
You pull away, using air from my lungs to
whisper low in my ear
And I am limitless.

When I am with you, I am beautiful,
so when you tell me so,
I just say thank you

Distance

It has been quite some time without now,
I sit on the sill, parched for even a drop
of water
of sunlight
of her real smile
of her bubbling laugh

Sacred earth round my roots
has gone dry,
lifelines shriveled in decay

My stem bends hard at my base,
and my flowerhead droops low in shame,
petals fraying like tissue paper,
crinkled and dead,
crisp at the ends

Without, I will wilt,
crumble to dust in the breeze
But I am not gone yet
and I will fight to stay

no, im feeling

shit.
shit.
closure.

late night love
somehow
fuck you
turned to
fuck me
somewhere
your sapphire eyes
wrap your arms around my waist

predisposed addiction
damn i never want rehab
every night is a new high to chase

i hate feeling

claiming to be strong, independent
writing love poetry about your ass
cant stop

pull me in for another kiss
only one piece left

shouldnt have it
diet.
stop?
absolutely not

savor every last bite you give
and i get you

Empty

What happens to the shell once the turtle dies?
Has anyone ever asked that question?
When they're alive, the brown, crusty exterior is
a part of the creature,
remove it, and you kill it.
But has anyone ever asked how the shell feels,
inevitably being separated from the one who
gave it life, gave it meaning?
Once the turtle perishes, what is the shell to
become?
A touch and play toy at some science center for
grabby, snotty children?
The grains of sand that aid newborns make it
back to sea?
A piece of rancid garbage disintegrating in a
landfill until it's nothing more than dust and
sludge?

I am the shell, and I have lost my turtle.
What am I to do with myself now?
What am I to become?
I've served my purpose,
or maybe I failed, and that's why my turtle is
gone?

I miss my turtle.
Each day I sit, cold and alone
and I yearn for the feeling of their heart beating
against my lower wall,
if I'm still enough, barely breathing, I can still
feel the faint thumping inside me
and how their skin and chapped, scaly limbs
embodied me
I was them, and they were me
We were one; symbiotic.

I am rotting without them,
decaying from the outside in as icy rain washes
over my rigid dome,
soon I will be nothing, a shell of a shell
My life ended with them, for now I am empty